THE UNEXPLAINED

IMAGINING OTHER WORLDS

Produced by Carlton Books Limited
20 Mortimer Street
London, W1N 7RD

First published in hardback edition in 2001 by Chelsea House Publishers, a subsidiary of
Haights Cross Communications. Printed and bound in Dubai.

First Printing
1 3 5 7 9 8 6 4 2

The Chelsea House World Wide Web address is http://www.chelseahouse.com

Library of Congress Cataloging-in-Publication Data applied for

Historic Realms of Marvels and Miracles ISBN: 0-7910-6076-4
Ancient Worlds, Ancient Mysteries ISBN: 0-7910-6077-2
Lost Worlds and Forgotten Secrets ISBN: 0-7910-6078-0
We Are Not Alone ISBN: 0-7910-6079-9
Imagining Other Worlds ISBN: 0-7910-6080-2
Coming from the Skies ISBN: 0-7910-6081-0
Making Contact ISBN: 0-7910-6082-9

THE ——
UNEXPLAINED

IMAGINING OTHER WORLDS

Where Faith and Fact Meet

Hilary Evans

Chelsea House Publishers

Philadelphia

THE
UNEXPLAINED

IMAGINING OTHER WORLDS

CONTENTS

Picturing The Martians

✴

Early in the morning of June 30, 1908, an enormous aerial explosion, visible from a distance of 800 km, flattened some 2000 km² of pine forest near the Tunguska River in central Siberia. Vast numbers of trees were knocked down, and because they all fell away from a central point, it was easy to identify that point as the epicentre. But there was nothing there, not even a crater, just a marshy bog. Witnesses spoke of a huge fireball, and the most probable explanation is that a comet fragment entered Earth's atmosphere. Being formed of ice and dust, it would disintegrate, creating a fireball and blast wave but no impact crater. Such is the scientific explanation for the unique "Tunguska Explosion". But because it is only a suggestion, alternative interpretations of the event have been proposed. Of these, the most intriguing is that the object which exploded in our atmosphere was not a natural object but an artifact – a spacecraft from another world.

ANCIENT ASTRONAUTS

A similar suggestion has been proposed to explain the Biblical account of the destruction of the cities of the plain, Sodom and Gomorrah. In 1960, a Russian professor named M M Agrest proposed that it had been caused not by "fire from Heaven" as the Bible suggests, but by a nuclear explosion generated by extraterrestrial invaders 5000 years ago.

Geologists offer more mundane explanations. Neev and Emery, in a 1995 study, pointed out that "the cities are in an earthquake-prone belt and their area has been subject to severe changes of climate lasting hundreds of years" – no need to look to other worlds for an explanation. But to support his thesis, Agrest pointed to the megalithic monuments of Baalbek, in the Lebanon, which he suggested might have been the launching platforms for interplanetary space ships.

Since then, the "ancient astronaut" concept has become a substantial sub-division of popular scientific speculation. Its champions point to the many

The heart of the devastation at Tunguska, where a huge area of forest was mysteriously flattened.

admittedly mysterious ruins and artifacts scattered about the world, and find explanations for all of them in terms of visits to our planet by otherworldly beings. Literally hundreds of books have been published with titles such as *"Extra-terrestrial Visitations from Prehistoric Times to the Present"*, *"Mankind – Child of the Stars"* or *"We are not the first"*. Far fewer books have been published exposing the weaknesses of the suggested scenarios.

Folklore seems to provide a legitimization of this approach. The mythologies of many cultures contain legends of a "Golden Age" preceding our present era, a time when people lived in peace and harmony with nature and with one another, when everything was better than it is now. The myths vary from one culture to another, but the fact that the idea is so widespread has encouraged some to think that even though its virtues may have been exaggerated, there really was some form of civilization before our own.

Speculation about these earlier societies has spawned a vast body of literature. Some of it involves great

LEFT: *With its big head and "wrap-around" eyes, Debbie Lee's classic "grey" represents aliens as perceived by witnesses of the 1980s/1990s.*

ABOVE: *Many believe something other than natural causes destroyed Sodom and Gomorrah.*
LEFT: *After 90 years, Tunguska still captures the imagination: a scene from the TV series,* The X-Files.

which seemed to give them substance. Von Däniken is given to such passages as this, taken almost at random from his writings:

> Could this gold plaque be a message from alien astronauts to us? Who will decipher this code? What has it got to tell us?

Though the French writer Paul Misraki (writing as "Paul Thomas") may have been the first non-fiction author to link the idea of flying saucers and "ancient astronauts", it was von Däniken whose series of best-selling books did most to popularize the notion that today's UFOs are only the latest in a long history of visits from other worlds. Many cultures have traditions of a god who imparted to them the secrets of art and civilization, such as the Central American deity Quetzalcoatl. Now, authors such as Maurice Chatelain (*"Our Ancestors Came from Outer Space"*) and Robert Charroux (*"Legacy of the Gods"*) proposed that those mythic gods were in fact visiting extraterrestrials, and devoted book after book to showing that "man's mysterious ancestry" had an otherworldly origin.

physical changes in the world. The notion that there formerly existed a large country, if not an entire continent, in the Atlantic, named Atlantis, is one theory. There are also good reasons to believe that something of the sort existed in the Pacific. A vast body of myth supports the idea of Mu, or Lemuria, where now there is empty ocean.

Such legends have been retold throughout human history. It is indisputable that cultures have come and gone in mankind's past, leaving behind monuments and other relics – Stonehenge, Baalbek, the Pyramids – which we do not fully understand. But only recently, with the beginning of our own first tentative explorations of space, has it been proposed that extraterrestrial visitors were involved.

The idea that beings from other planets might have visited Earth before the birth of humanity is not a new one. As is so often the case, science fiction writers got there first. In the November 1934 issue of *Wonder Stories*, Philip Barshafsky tells a story of a Martian landing on Earth during the Jurassic Era. Mars itself is becoming unfit for habitation, and the invaders are one of a succession of expeditions sent to other planets to see if any of them might provide suitable colonies for the Martians to resettle. Earth alone, they find, is suitable, or would be, were it not for the dinosaurs. For a while the superior technology of the Martians enables them to hold off the attacks of the huge animals, but eventually brute force wins the day. The Martians are annihilated, their spaceship rusts away and nothing is left to show that aliens had ever set foot on our planet.

The scenarios sketched by Swiss author Erich von Däniken and the other theorists of twenty years later were somewhat different, but by then flying saucers had appeared on the scene. Authors such as Brinsley Le Poer Trench, Lord Clancarty, were inspired by the thought that today's flying saucers were part of an on-going tradition of extraterrestrial visitation. While the theories were no less speculative than the science fiction, their creators stirred fact into their speculation in a way

The Great Temple at Baalbek is so impressive that some writers insist aliens were responsible.

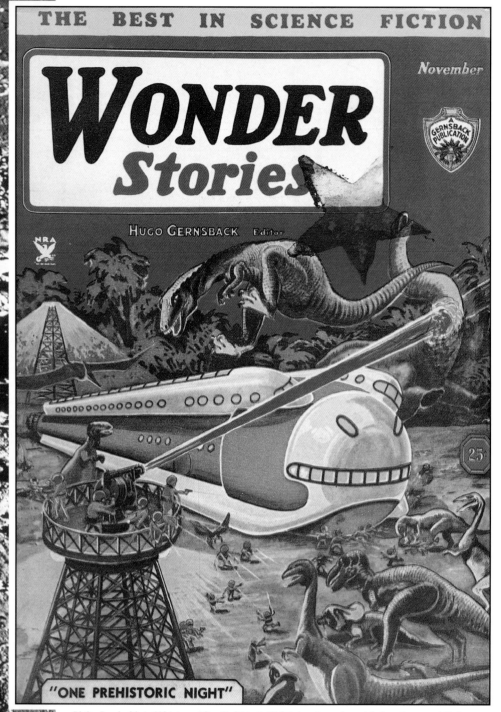

THE BEST IN SCIENCE FICTION

November

WONDER Stories

HUGO GERNSBACK Editor

"ONE PREHISTORIC NIGHT"

Philip Barshofsky's 1934 story, "One Prehistoric Night", imagines what might have happened if aliens had landed on Earth during the age of the dinosaurs.

Scattered about our planet are a number of objects – ranging from small artifacts to vast building complexes, from massive markings on the ground to enigmatic drawings on cave walls – which can be interpreted as evidence that our planet has housed other civilizations preceding our own. Just how bold these hypotheses can be is illustrated by Robert Charroux, perhaps the least inhibited of the ancient astronaut proponents:

We have evidence that interplanetary rockets streaked across the heavens millions of years ago; that atomic bombs destroyed one or more civilizations; that extraterrestrials left traces of their presence in several parts of our planet; that Moses was familiar with explosives and a death ray; that a man lighted his house with electricity in the time of Saint Louis; that an aeroplane flew during the reign of John V of Portugal; that secret societies forged the destiny of mankind …

The clever part is devising a single, coherent story which will embrace all these dispersed and disparate items. A number of alternative scenarios are currently on offer. Though each has its individual features, they can be roughly classified into groups:

- Humankind of a sort already existed, but we were incapable of development on our own. We required guidance from more advanced, extraterrestrial, civilizations to set us on the right track. In some scenarios, this guidance was limited to instruction; in others, genetic manipulation was required to enable man to climb a rung of the evolutionary ladder. In yet others, cross-breeding was required to let early humans acquire the genetic components necessary to become civilized creatures.
- We humans developed our own civilization, but the process was covertly masterminded by the more advanced extraterrestrials, in much the same fashion as a farmer oversees his livestock.
- We developed our own civilization, but things went wrong, so the extraterrestrials, in the spirit of cosmic co-operation, intervened to save us from the consequences of our mistakes.
- Humanity itself is of extraterrestrial origin, the Earth having been colonized by extraterrestrial explorers from whom we are descended.

Such speculation has often been widely dismissed as irresponsible, and unquestionably a lot of nonsense has been written. Nevertheless, these theories have opened our eyes to possibilities we might not otherwise have entertained, inviting us to set our imaginations loose on the origin and nature of the universe. However silly many of the ideas may be, they remind us how much is still unknown about the early history of humanity.

But precisely because so little is known, it is difficult for these speculations to find confirmation. The theories flourish, but their roots are shallow. Though some proponents of the ancient astronaut hypothesis have sought to find a historical basis for their suggestions in legendary writings, this is never more than speculation based on interpretation of such passages as this:

> And it came to pass, when men began to multiply on the face of the earth, and daughters were born unto them, that the sons of God saw the daughters of men that they were fair; and they took them wives of all which they chose… and also after that, when the sons of God came in unto the daughters of men, and they bare children to them, the same became mighty men which were of old, men of renown.
>
> **GENESIS 6**

Certainly, a case can be made out that by "the sons of God" extraterrestrial beings are meant, but equally the reference may simply be to a terrestrial legend.

OUR AIRBORNE ANCESTORS

Whichever "Ancient Astronaut" scenario we adopt, we must suppose that they travelled here in a spacecraft of some kind. Then they either flew away again or, if they remained here, they destroyed their vessels, as Cortes burned his boats on the shores of Mexico so his men would not be tempted to sail back to Spain.

Several believers in "nuts and bolts' UFOs, keen to shore up their belief that it isn't simply a "space-age myth", have sought to establish a prehistory of the UFO. In his 1953 book *Flying Saucers Have Landed*, Desmond Leslie writes:

> For as long as man has been able to write and record things he has periodically noted the passage of luminous discs and fiery spindle-shaped objects in our skies. In ancient Rome, many references were made to "Flying Shields" … In China they were called "fiery dragons" … Frescoes in a fourteenth-century Yugoslavian church show little men in space capsules … Inscriptions on ancient stones depict spacecraft of the disk and spindle variety. There are cave drawings of men in curious looking spacesuits, almost indentical with the garb worn by modern astronauts.

Even if these interpretations are

correct, they do not prove that there was any intereaction with Earthpeople: still less do they give any support to: "ancient astronaut" theories.

The Bible is a favourite hunting ground for early spacecraft. Numerous incidents, especially in the Old Testament, have been re-interpreted as UFO events: the vision of Ezeikel is a classic example and any reference to "fiery chariots" is taken to be UFOs.

In June 1974, businessman Charles Silva had an interesting experience in Peru: in his book *Date with the Gods* he describes meeting an extraterrestrial calling herself Rama, who explains that she is on a mission to Earth to save humanity. When three flying saucers cross the sky, she tells him not to be

surprised – "I see them all the time," she tells him, "They're all over the world." Then she adds, "If you want to know about flying saucers, the bible is the place to go. There's a lot of evidence of flying objects in its pages." In the course of several meetings, she explains to him how extraterrestrials have been visiting Earth through human history. And they still are – for Silva himself sees them and communicates with them telepathically.

If Silva, and others have had similar encounters, can be believed, then this is valuable evidence for the prehistory of UFOs. But can we believe them? Is Silva's story fact or fiction? As we shall see later, it is not always easy to tell one from the other.

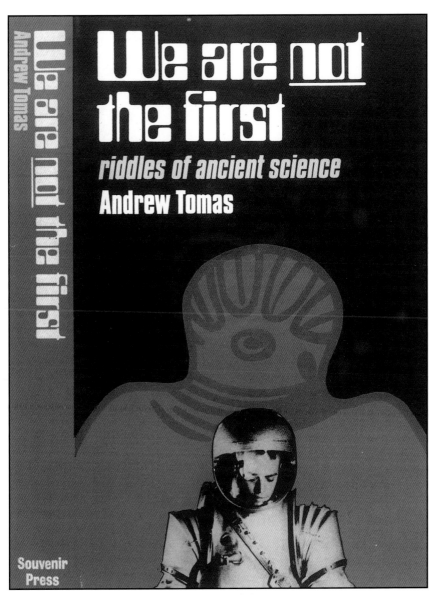

Andrew Tomas was one of the first writers to propose that "ancient astronauts" visited our planet in prehistoric times.

CHARIOTS OF THE GODS?

ERICH VON DANIKEN

Unsolved mysteries of the past
ERICH VON DANIKEN

PHYSICAL EVIDENCE

Since so much remains unknown about humanity's distant past, it is often impossible to prove that the champions of the Ancient Astronaut theories are mistaken. Generally, it's a question of comparing their explanation to the conventional one, and choosing the more acceptable. Sometimes, though, it is possible to demonstrate the weakness of their reasoning. For example, the construction of the Pyramids, the buildings of Baalbek and the erection of the sculptured figures on Easter Island are all said by these writers to be beyond the skills available to our ancestors. This suggests that they were perhaps instructed in the appropriate technology by extraterrestrial visitors, or even that the visitors were themselves responsible for the constructions.

However, in all three of the instances cited above, it has been shown that the constructions *could* have been carried out by techniques involving comparatively simple skills which we can imagine our ancestors using. Thor Heyerdahl, notably, carried out experiments on Easter Island showing that, though erecting those massive figures calls for considerable ingenuity, it requires no sophisticated technology. While such demonstrations do not prove that these techniques were employed, their existence makes it gratuitous to invoke extraterrestrial assistance.

One of the most notorious of the artifacts produced as evidence for visits by "ancient astronauts" is the carved stone lid of a sarcophagus in a temple at Palenque, Mexico, discovered by the Mexican archaeologist Lhuillier in 1949. Two French authors, Tarade and Millou, noted the resemblance to the pilot of a rocket-ship, and the suggestion was taken up enthusiastically by others. Raymond A Drake, for example, writes: "There seems little doubt that it represents anything other than a humanoid piloting a rocket, even though it was

Discovered in 1949, this carving on a Mayan sarcophagus has been interpreted as depicting a space traveller, though in fact it is a typical example of Mayan religious art.

LEFT: *Erich von Däniken caught the world's imagination with his claims that extraterrestrials have visited Earth throughout human history.*

carved thousands of years ago". In fact, it wasn't much over one thousand – the date carved on the tomb is the equivalent of AD 612.

Von Däniken adopted the idea, without drawing attention to the fact that the tomb in fact is not a unique object. There are many similar artifacts, though no other is quite so striking. The scene is a religious one, embodying common motifs of Mayan religious art.

Dr Peter White, Lecturer in Prehistory at the University of Sydney, says of it "This scene is repeated elsewhere in Mayan carvings ... it embodies various beliefs about the world and the after-world" and comments:

If we are dealing with an astronaut in a rocket, how does it come to be so like our own rockets in shape and propulsion? If the earth is being regularly visited by

astronauts as part of an interstellar experiment, then surely we would expect the spaceships to be rather more developed, to use an atomic or magnetic drive on their inter-galactic jaunts, to be pollution-free and computerized. Why is the Palenque astronaut using a superannuated Saturn Rocket?

Wall paintings at Tassili n'Ajjer in the Algerian Sahara – discovered by French archaeologist Henri Lhote in 1956, and dating from between 8000–6000 BC – have also been claimed by writers as "space-suited figures". We are invited to suppose that our ancestors drew pictures of visiting extraterrestrials of long ago, just as they did the bison and deer of the Lascaux cave-paintings. Certainly there is a superficial resemblance, but as critic Ronald Story points out, it is rather odd that the aliens would wear space helmets yet be otherwise naked. Many have their sexual organs exposed, which to anthropologists suggests that they are intended to depict the ritual figures of fertility cults. The same is true of wall paintings in Uzbekistan in the former Soviet Union and elsewhere. In the absence of any direct evidence linking them to extraterrestrial visitors, and with good reason to suggest a more

human explanation, they hardly constitute persuasive proof that they represent long-ago alien visitors.

Often, too, the champions of the Ancient Astronaut theories distort the facts to suit their purpose. The Nazca lines in Peru admittedly present a genuine mystery. Though many explanations have been proposed, the enigma remains unresolved. Von Däniken argues that, since the lines are clearly designed to be seen from the air, this implies that they were made for or by extraterrestrial visitors. But while it may well be that the markings are intended to be seen from the air, this could have been simply a "message" to the gods in the same way that many of us pray to our gods. It does not imply that extraterrestrials were physically present, still less that they were responsible for them. Von Däniken reproduces a photograph of the Nazca lines, but gives no indication of scale. It seems to back his suggestion that the lines could have been a landing field for extraterrestrial spacecraft until we realize that the scale has been deceptively exaggerated. This is quite apart from the many reasons for questioning whether extraterrestrial visitors would need a landing-strip, any more than we did when we visited the Moon.

This drawing at Tassili n'Ajjer is seen by some writers as "the Great Martian God", though anthropologists view it as a fertility-figure.

Another form of evidence concerns the possession of sophisticated knowledge. Thus NASA engineer Maurice Chatelain has made the striking discovery that lines drawn between (some of) the great French cathedrals, many, though not all, of which are dedicated to the Virgin Mary, match – provided one employs a flat projection – the constellation of Virgo. For Chatelain, this is evidence of a knowledge of astronomy far greater than that known to have been possessed at that time – knowledge which, he suggests, can only be of extraterrestrial origin. Exactly why the cathedral planners wished to reflect the celestial layout is something we can only wonder about.

Certainly, the more we uncover our past, the more reason we find to admire the skills of our ancestors. Patterns emerge to show that the positioning of a stone or the alignment of a monument may be design rather than chance. However, as has been shown in numerous examples, from the authorship of Shakespeare to the recently discovered "Bible Code", a combination of chance with careful selection of instances will

ABOVE: *The Great Pyramid and the Sphinx have attracted more theories than any other monuments.*
LEFT: *The stone figures of Easter Island were thought by some to be evidence of alien technology.*

The destruction of Mu: the author James Churchward claimed in his book The Lost Continent of Mu *that the great Pacific continent was overwhelmed by a combination of flood and volcanic action.*

often suffice to explain the apparent demonstration, particularly when the claims are hedged about with many limiting conditions, as in Chatelain's example. That esoteric knowledge was employed is very likely, for skilled craftsmen tend to jealously guard their trade secrets, but such circumstantial evidence offers feeble grounds for invoking otherworldly visitors.

ANCIENT WISDOM

There are many traditions that there exists a body of ancient wisdom, running counter to established religious or scientific views, which has been secretly preserved by a succession of privileged adepts. Roger Bacon, Sir Francis Bacon, Nikolas Tesla and even Einstein are among those cited as Illuminati or "Lords of the Flame" working secretly in our midst. Robert Charroux asserts that there is,

a conspiracy of initiates whose purpose was to keep the people of the world in ignorance of their ancestors" prodigious adventure ... The conspiracy must have existed for at least six thousand years, doling out such scientific knowledge as men could safely assimilate, but holding back what could not be divulged without danger.

Charroux and other theorists suggest that powers such as astral projection, telepathy, psychokinesis and psychic healing, which we tend to label paranormal, were commonly possessed by our ancestors who obtained them from extraterrestrials. But even if we accept that such phenomena occur, the idea that otherworldly visitors are responsible is pure speculation. There have always been secret societies, but there are no grounds for supposing that they derived their knowledge from otherworldly sources. Moreover, these authors are remarkably reticent in providing useful details of their sources. James Churchward, who has resolutely promoted the concept of a Pacific continent of Mu in a series of books

in which "fact" is piled tirelessly on "fact", claims to have received his private information while staying in "certain Monasteries in India and Tibet whose names are withheld by request".

There are in fact sound geophysical reasons for believing that some such continent formerly existed, but Churchward arouses suspicion rather than trust when he is so coy about his sources. Similarly, George Hunt Williamson, offering us some very esoteric ideas "linking ancient civilizations and the mysteries of their temple rituals with the remote beginnings of humanity and visitations from Outer Space", bases his theories on information obtained

from very ancient manuscripts preserved in the great library of one of the world's time-honoured mystery schools, a 'lost city' high in the mountains of Peru. In this city lives a master teacher, a survivor of the Elders ...

But he does not tell us what manuscripts, which master teacher, which mystery school, or which "lost" city …

Peter Kolosimo, writing of the tunnel built by extraterrrestrials under the Pacific from Asia to America, says

lamas who have been questioned about the tunnels have usually replied, "Yes, they exist: they were made by giants who gave us the benefit of their knowledge when the world was young".

Unfortunately he does not tell us

which lamas, who they were speaking to, when and where they said so, or how dependable these commentators were on other matters.

These authors are entertaining to read and provide legitimate food for thought. Though they select only what serves their purpose, and exaggerate its significance, they frequently draw our attention to genuine puzzles. They invite us to question establishment explanations and received opinions. But without the backing of solid

evidence, their speculations have little more substance than the fantasies of the authors of popular science fiction short stories.

EXOTIC VARIATIONS

In addition to the various general themes, there have been any number of specific accounts. The thesis presented by Zecharia Sitchin in *The Twelfth Planet* and developed in later works is characteristic of the genre. Sitchin, like the ancient astronaut proponents, and like theological commentators for centuries before, had been puzzled by references to the Nephilim – the giant offspring of the unnatural union between visiting "sons of the Gods" and the "daughters of men" – who figure in the Bible and other Middle Eastern traditions. How was it possible, he asked, for these beings to come and go so frequently between Earth and their home? The implication, he felt, was that they must have come from nearby.

He agreed with orthodox science that none of the existing planets in the solar system was a suitable candidate, but produced legends which point to the existence of a twelfth planet, Marduk, whose orbit brings it close to Earth every 3600 years. Some 450,000 years ago its inhabitants took advantage of a close orbit to land and colonize our planet, and eventually, needing a slave race to do their dirty work, they created mankind. Unfortunately humanity didn't turn out to be quite the obedient second-class citizens they had in mind, so our visitors left, expecting us to be wiped out by the tidal waves caused by the reappearance of the twelfth planet. However, they didn't reckon on Noah and his Ark.

Catastrophe of a different kind was involved in the story told by the Mann family from Gloucestershire, England, who reported being taken aboard a spaceship from Janos on June 19, 1978. Their abductors explained to them, in a scenario diametrically opposed to Sitchin's, that they themselves are the descendants of Earthpeople! Long, long ago, colonists from our planet had

Sir Francis Bacon, whose vast learning and far-sighted ideas have caused him to be thought of as a master of secret knowledge in a great occult tradition.

The "humming-bird" image, preserved for centuries on the arid plains of Nazca, Peru, and seemingly intended to be seen from the air.

developed the technology to travel in space. They had settled elsewhere in the universe, including Janos, a planet several thousand light years from Earth. Unfortunately, their home had come under threat of imminent destruction by natural forces, and they had to take refuge aboard giant spaceships. Now these prodigals were asking if we would take them back? Overpopulated our planet may be, they understood, but surely we could find room for them somewhere? Norway, for instance, didn't seem particularly overcrowded, and there were only 10 million of them, drifting around the solar system in their saucers like planes stacked above an airport, waiting for permission to land.

Frank Johnson presented his account of "The Janos People" in 1980, and since then nothing has been heard of them, to my knowledge. Presumably they are still out there, wandering about the skies, extraterrestrial refugees. Maybe some other planet has been more welcoming.

Although every year new theories of this kind are published, the failure of their inventors to establish any firm basis for extraterrestrial visitation has resulted in a general tendency to put the ideas on hold. Several sceptical books have been published which demonstrate the weakness of the theories. Though these counter-claims did not get onto the best-seller lists, they have had a general effect of discouraging people from accepting the claims literally.

In short, the case is not proven. The mysteries are there, no question. The Nazca Lines, Stonehenge and many other artifacts continue to challenge us. But the fact that we cannot explain them in the light of our current knowledge does not mean that we should invoke beings from other worlds, for there is not a scrap of evidence that they are responsible. Our remote ancestors, when they did not understand the thunder, attributed it to the anger of the gods. We have now abandoned that

explanation, but, it seems, we are still disposed to look beyond this world to explain what we can't understand.

WHAT HAPPENED TO THE ASTRONAUTS?

Even if beings from other worlds visited our planet in the remote past, they evidently did not choose to settle here, or, if they did, they were wiped out. This calamity not only destroyed them but must have removed every trace of them, their activities and their handiwork, beyond a few controversial monuments.

Not everyone agrees. Some have suggested that they *did* remain in some form. In a 1957 book, the American writer Morris Jessup speculated:

There are "little people" in African and

New Guinea jungles today … but *nobody* knows their origin or ancestry. Were these isolated tribes "planted" in the tropical jungle from UFO thousands of years ago? Did UFO land, or crash, and establish racial germs or colonies?

In support of this somewhat improbable suggestion, he cited a newspaper story:

> During construction work on the Cathedral of Saint John (New York), workmen left a high scaffold in place over a weekend. When they returned, they found lying on the scaffolding the body of a little man with one eye in the middle of his forehead. A New York *Times* reporter is said to have written it up, but his story was "killed" to avoid the charge of sensationalism. Army authorities were said to have removed the body.

Jessup does not tell us what makes him leap immediately to the idea that this "little man" should be a solitary survivor from a race of prehistoric alien visitors. But in any case it is a big leap from pigmies surviving in remote jungle areas to god-like alien beings revered as the bringers of art and civilization.

This and other intriguing scenarios each have their champions, but they remain unsupported speculation. It seems more likely that, if there ever were any "ancient astronauts", they didn't like our planet enough to want to stay here. For all practical purposes, any question of visitors to Earth before human history must be placed in the "pending" file until some really convincing evidence turns up.

THE STAR PEOPLE

During the 1980s, new claims were made that otherworldly people were present on Earth, but this time the scenario was a very different one. It was revealed that thousands, perhaps millions of people who appear to be normal human beings are, in fact, extraterrestrials.

The most visible exponent of this notion has been the American writer Brad Steiger. He, both alone and in collaboration with his wife Francie, has authored a series of books stating that many people on Earth are extraterrestrials, though they may not always realize it.

The concept did not originate with the Steigers, of course. The idea of extraterrestrials mixing with humans and living among us may be as old as the Bible, and has surfaced over and over again in different contexts. Self-proclaimed alien contactees Howard Menger and his wife Connie are two of the most prominent to claim an extraterrestrial origin – he from Saturn, she from Venus. Author Dana Howard, too, considers herself an "Earthborn Venusian" and in addition to telling of her own adventures *("She came from Venus")* has written a fiction story in which her Venusian heroine becomes the first woman president of the United States.

The contactee phenomenon seems to have been one of individuals who were selected because of their personal qualities. This was certainly the case so far as Dana Howard and the Mengers are concerned. But by the 1990s, the notion of a chosen elite had given place to a collective phenomenon. As abductions escalated from isolated cases to thousands, and then to millions, so more and more people came to realize that they, too, were "Star People".

In his 1995 book *From elsewhere: being E.T. in America*, Dr Scott Mandelker invited his readers to contemplate the fact that:

> There may be as many as 100 million extraterrestrials living on Earth. Most of them are what could be called Sleeping Wanderers.

The number is not mere guesswork, but was arrived at as a result of channelled messages received from the extraterrestrials themselves, and they should know. Mandelker explains that by "Wanderers" he means:

> … those E.T. souls who have been extraterrestrial since birth, but who've forgotten who they are and live under a kind of veil of their true being, and then slowly – if they're fortunate – begin to awaken.

The Wanderers are born, like Jesus, of human parents. Some may never come to realize their extraterrestrial origins, though this seems rather a waste of their talents since they are here on our planet to carry out a mission. Those who have not yet awakened to their extraterrestrial origin are known as "Sleeping Wanderers", which makes them sound more like zombies than emissaries of a superior race. It is not clear who gave them these labels, whether they are Mandelker's own invention or is what these people call themselves. Although Steiger writes the introduction to Mandelker's book, the author does not seem to have felt the need to retain Steiger's "Star People" label.

The Earth-born Wanderers are not the only kind of aliens living in our midst. There is also another category, the "Walk-ins". These are "real" aliens of extraterrestrial origin who have taken over the physical bodies of Earthpeople, who voluntarily relinquish life on this planet in favour of life elsewhere, for a time at least.

So what are all these extraterrestrials doing on our planet? They are here to help us. Unlike the aggressive abductors we shall be meeting later, these are benevolent citizens of the cosmos who are altruistically concerned at the way our Earthly civilization is developing, and who have come among us to help us from the inside. This has been going on throughout history – Americans will be proud to know that Benjamin Franklin and Thomas Jefferson were both extraterrestrials. On the other hand, it could be said that if the representatives of these superior civilizations are here to help our ailing Earth, they are certainly taking their time about it.

The curious thing about the Star People is that they don't immediately know that that is what they are. They have to find out. Sometimes finding out comes in the form of a revelation from "the Beyond", sometimes from a vision. Presumably quite a high proportion learn of their true nature by reading books like The *Star People* by Brad and Francie Steiger, which says on its cover:

> IMAGINE THE JOY OF FINDING OUT THAT YOU ARE ONE OF THE **STAR PEOPLE!**

It is, evidently, a joyful discovery. You

0-425-05513-2 · $2.75 · A BERKLEY BOOK

IMAGINE THE JOY OF FINDING OUT THAT YOU ARE ONE OF

THE STAR PEOPLE

BRAD & FRANCIE STEIGER

The startling truth about the thousands of "aliens" now awakening among us!

learn that, as you always suspected, you are not quite like other people: you are someone special, in fact you are someone superior. You are not here on Earth simply to be a population statistic, but to fulfil a high purpose, that of saving the Earth!

Still, it does seem rather remarkable that, with so important a mission to accomplish, those whose function is to carry out that mission should learn of their role in such a haphazard, uncertain way. Steiger tells us:

> Ever since I was a child, I have felt as though I were really a stranger here on Earth. I felt that I was an observer, rather than a participant, of this alien land in which I found myself.

And his wife Francie says:

> I believe I am one of the Star People. When I was 4$^{1}/_{2}$ years old, two men, one dark-haired and the other blond, came up to me. These mysterious messengers told me I was here on earth for a special mission that I would come to understand later in life.

It seems a very casual method of recruitment. You might think it would be better to be sure. In fact, though, most of those who have come to consider themselves Star People *are* certain of it because they have had some experience that proves it, at any rate so far as they are concerned. A good many of them were told the good news by an apparition of some kind. For Dr G H, a psychologist from Texas, it was an angel; for C L, a teacher from Arizona, it appeared to be a Native American; S S, a New York psychotherapist, learnt it from a goddess named Bast; while P B, a Pennsylvania psychiatrist, encountered a beautifully robed entity who seemed to be Jesus.

These entities are not necessarily who they seem to be. H L L of California had a vision of Jesus at age 11, but:

> I realized later that it was actually a guide who appeared to me as Jesus, because at that time I was very religious and would only accept a guide in that

FROM
ELSEWHERE
BEING E.T. IN AMERICA

"FASCINATING RESEARCH...IMPECCABLY DONE... A TOPIC NO ONE ELSE HAS DARED TO TOUCH." —Kenneth Ring, Ph.D., author of *The Omega Project*

ARE YOU—
OR IS SOMEONE
YOU KNOW—
AN E.T.?

Scott Mandelker, Ph.D.

With an Introduction by Brad Steiger

Like the Steigers, Scott Mandelker reveals that he himself is an extraterrestrial, one of millions who have been sent to help the people of Earth.

form. The entity used big words which I could not understand at that time, but I remembered them until I could. The gist of what he said was that I was to grow to become aware of all things.

Certainly the Star People do seem to possess exceptional talents. Few people can remember words they do not understand, even less if they heard

them at an early age. They seem to live more deeply than most of us, even when young: Professor Leo Sprinkle of Laramie, Wyoming, an investigator who came to realize that he is himself a Star Person, tells us that:

> at five or six, I felt a "pull" toward another world, as if I had a mission to accomplish here before I could rejoin my

"true home". I was sad and apprehensive in my task.

Because Star People are as precocious in their feelings as in their intelligence, it is perhaps not surprising that so many of them are visited by their guides at a very tender age and told that when they are adult they will understand. It seems a rather odd procedure, but doubtless it serves some purpose, if only to make it less of a shock when they are subsequently briefed on their role.

Interestingly, this is something the Star People have in common with the majority of the UFO contactees and abductees. Many of them, too, receive "previews" during childhood of their later role as involuntary guests of the aliens. This may, of course, be what it seems to be, the otherworldly forces making sure of their human associates. On the other hand, a psychologist might think that if all these people share this experience of childhood conditioning, it is because they share a common psychological disposition. Whether that disposition is bestowed on them by the aliens or springs from the depths of their personalities is another question.

Most extraterrestrials on Earth who have come to realize their true nature are convinced that they have a mission to accomplish. One that I met personally told me she had exchanged bodies some years earlier with a 12-year old Earth girl because she had a vital mission to carry out. She was the captain of a crew, a role whose job description sounded very similar to that of James Kirk, captain of *Star Trek*'s "Enterprise". Indeed, I was privileged to be present when she was reunited with a member of her crew, a Texan lady who was attending the same get-together. The two ladies immediately recognized each other as ETs, which was nice. She told me, not without humour, about the difficulties of adjusting from being an ET to being an Earth person. But there are compensations, it seems. Another Star Person, Inid, says that the human sex procedure is one of the "perks" of being incarnate in a physical Earthly body.

Some Wanderers have very specific roles to play. Vikram was attending a

channelling meeting when he suddenly realized that he was a member of the Council of Twelve that the speaker was channelling a message about. The Council of Twelve is connected with Ashtar Command, an extraterrestrial organization which has many links to Earthpeople – a well-known American contactee, George Van Tassel of California, was privileged to receive many messages from the same source, and other contactees have claimed the same privilege. Inid, the alien who finds Earth sex such fun, is certain that "at one time, she was the sole representative on Earth of a confederation of extraterrestrial races".

What seems odd, though, is that – setting aside the references to Franklin and Jefferson – none of these Star People seem to be actually doing anything to justify their claim to be on a mission. Here they are, supposed to be saving our planet, and, according to Mandelker:

> ...for these people, time is spent ...[engaging in] reading, meditation, channelling, group membership, personal spiritual exploration ...these were the activities that I heard mentioned most often. About a third of those I spoke with said they felt closer to nature, even to animal and plant life, than they did to people. And about a third of those who hail From Elsewhere surprised me by stating they simply didn't feel very connected to people at all and didn't think much about it. They enjoy their solitude and have no deep yearning for personal relations.

This is all very well for the spiritual development of the individual Star Persons, but it doesn't sound as if it's going to help our planet very much. Mandelker tells us that there is a tendency for the Wanderers, once they become aware of their destiny, to move into caring professions like social work and teaching. Well, that's better than making bombs and killing people, but is it really worth coming all the way from a distant planet just to become a social worker on Earth?

Interestingly, though, this again mirrors very closely the experiences of many alien abductees as well. Back in 1980, during the early days of abductions,

American authors Judith and Alan Gansberg made a study of the after-effects of being abducted. They found a strong tendency for abductees to direct their lives towards healing, teaching, and caring. This is certainly borne out by those that I have met personally. John and Sue Day, who were abducted at Aveley, England, on October 27, 1974, experienced similar after-effects. John had a breakdown and had to give up his job, eventually finding more congenial work helping the mentally handicapped. He took to writing poems, gave up smoking, and became a vegetarian. His wife Sue followed a similar course of changed life.

Mandelker also tells of two women who shared an apartment in San Francisco. Although both were lesbians, they were not on good terms. However, both were undergoing past-life therapy, and among the revelations each experienced was the realization that they were both extraterrestrials. It proved to be a bond between them, enabling them to enter a shared relationship, and their former mutual hostility turned into a love affair. Once again, one has to comment that this may have been wonderful for them, but was it for this that they were sent to Earth?

How do you know if you are an extraterrestrial? Steiger and Mandelker both provide lists of the tell-tale clues, and other lists have appeared elsewhere. Here are some of the indicators. You are most likely a Star Person if:

- You feel somehow "different" from others
- You find life on Earth boring and meaningless
- You dreamed about UFOs and space as a child
- Your family have always thought you were "a bit odd"
- You feel your parents aren't your true parents
- You are not interested in money
- You see good in people, to the point of being naive
- You sincerely wish to improve the world
- You easily get lost in fantasy fiction

RIGHT: *John and Susan Day were abducted, with their child and their car, taken aboard a UFO, and subjected to an examination by the aliens.*

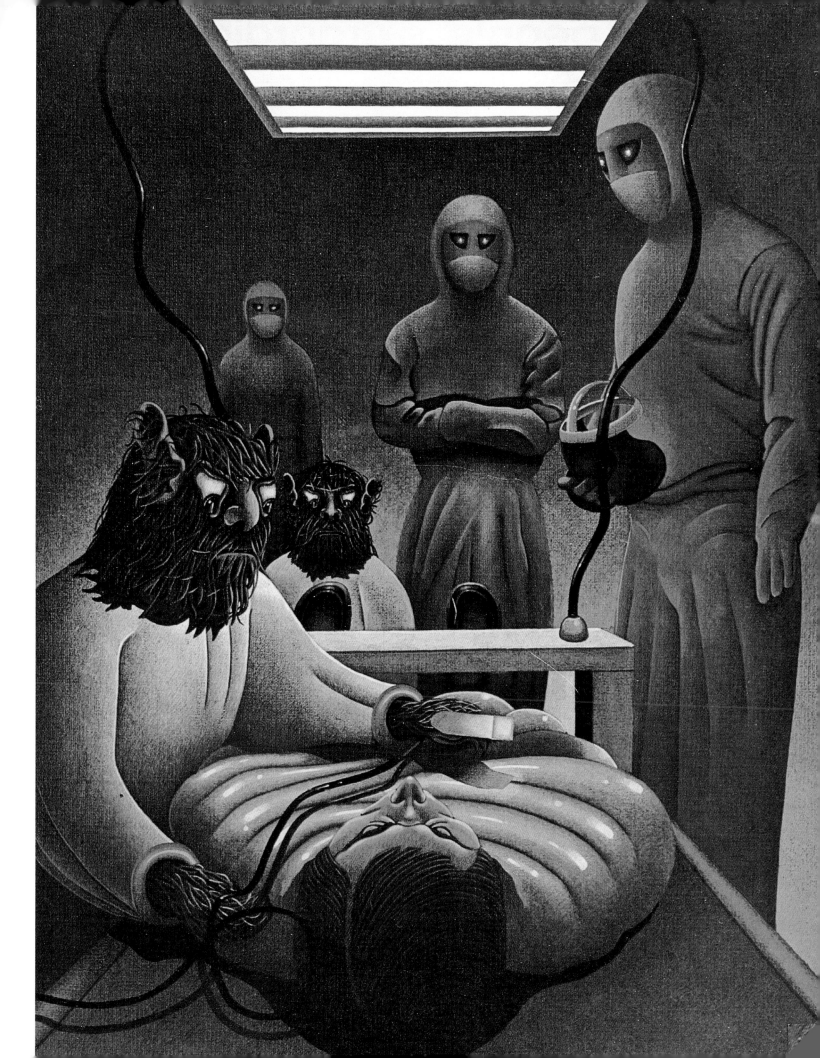

- You feel drawn towards Atlantis, Lemuria and other civilizations
- You are interested in enhancing your spiritual powers
- You don't require as much sleep as most people
- You are hypersensitive
- You are subject to headaches and migraines
- You had unseen friends as a child
- You seem to recall previous lives

Steiger himself, as we have noted, felt early in life that he was somehow "different" and this led to the realization that he is a Star Person. He was lucky enough to meet and marry another. Fellow-author Scott Mandelker, too, has come to recognize that he is one himself. When we look at contactee and abduction experiences, we shall see that many who investigate abductions discover, in the course of investigating the experiences of others, that they themselves have been abducted.

However, because identifying yourself as a Star Person is very much up to the individual – how do you define "feeling different from others" when each of us is unique? Many Wanderers do not feel totally confident that they are extraterrestrials. There is no exclusive biological indicator such as pointed ears or webbed feet which would at once settle the matter; instead, what is felt is a "subjective certainty". Unfortunately, while this may satisfy the individual concerned, it is not likely to carry conviction with others – unless, of course, they are themselves extraterrestrial.

This realization that one is a Star Person comes as a result of a process very similar to that of religious conversion – a similarity we shall notice in other contexts. It varies with the circumstances of the individual, ranging from a gradual realization that they are "not like other people" to a sudden flash of

recognition. However, as William James observed
in connection with religious conversion, even when there seems to be a sudden moment of recognition, there has generally been a long process of subconscious development before the realization comes to the surface. Clearly, this ties in with the childhood conditioning we have already noticed.

THE LORDS OF FLAME

If we go along with these people's claims that they have extraterrestrial origins, we have to ask "Where do they come from?" It turns out that they all come from actual civilizations on other worlds. Various locations are mentioned. Betty is from Antares in the Scorpio constellation, but with a base station on Venus. Julie and Linda are both from

... and in that moment he knew he was a Space Brother sent to awaken humanity

"A Space Brother sent to awaken humanity". Illustrator Gwen Fulton pokes gentle fun at the "Star People".

Sirius. But who, precisely, is master-minding the operation? There are references to a Council that meets on Saturn. One has a picture of the various members of the Council arriving in their spaceships, like earth committee members in their chauffeur-driven cars, and congregating in some celestial board-room. But probably it isn't like that. If these people are so much more technologically advanced than us, they would not need to "meet" anywhere. Virtual conferencing via computer should make a physical assembly unnecessary. Those who manage the Universe will do so without needing to leave their home planets.

The Star People seem to be assigned guides, who have the job, first, of telling them during childhood of their future mission, and then reinforcing that assurance when necessary. But they are never very explicit about who they are, they don't say exactly where in the universe they come from, and they are disturbingly vague about what they have in mind for Earth.

However benevolent these aliens may be, there is no assurance that they really know what is best for us Earthpeople. There is always the possibility that what they say doesn't reflect their real intentions, that this is in fact the beginning of a sinister plot to take over the Earth.

Some Star People have received insights concerning the ultimate authority behind the project. Dr Elsa von Eckartsberg – who has an impressive work-load teaching German, Comparative Literature, Psycho-synthesis and Stress-management at Harvard – comes from Venus, and is confident that we Earthpeople will connect ourselves to "the cosmic dimensions" in not too distant a future. She believes that "The Lords of Flame" projected sparks of consciousness into mindless men and awakened the intellect within them.

This takes us back to the Ancient Astronauts, and the ancient legends of gods who brought knowledge of the arts and civilization to mankind. One of the great enigmas of life is how and when Man developed the self-consciousness which distinguishes him from all other living creatures. Some proponents of the "ancient astronauts" scenario credit extraterrestrials with this achievement, and if Dr von Eckartsberg is correct, they are right to do so. It wasn't the result of evolution, it was literally a gift from the Gods. In which case, it is they who are responsible for the fact that things haven't turned out as well as they might. Perhaps that is why they feel the need to send missionaries to our planet to get us back onto the right track.

According to Brad and Francie Steiger, the ancestors of the Star People first came to Earth about 40,000 BC During most of that time they kept a close control over human activities. It was only during the last 4000 years – what we think of as recorded history, in fact – that we have been left to run our own lives, for better or worse. Unfortunately, this means that there is no historical record of their existence. We have to rely on what people like Francie Steiger tell us.

Fortunately, if there's one thing the Star People are happy to do, it is to give us messages from the Beyond, even though they are usually sadly short on fact and often contradict one another. Francie Steiger tells us that what happened to the aliens was that they "etherealized" into "pure energy". We are told that "they joyously accepted their elevation from physically dense matter to a finer vibratory frequency". They were not so preoccupied with their newly found transcendence that they neglected their responsibility towards the Earthpeople however. This is why people like her and Brad Steiger and Scott Mandelker have been sent, to "accelerate the process for the dwellers of Earth" so that we too may rise to a higher and less material state.

We have already noted similarities between the Star People's experiences and those of contactees and abductees. There are similarities of a different kind with other types of experience. The seeing of visions, for one, is a frequent accompaniment to religious conversion, and to the lives of individuals, such as Saint Teresa of Avila, who are called to a higher life of religious mysticism. Visions seem to play very much the same role in both cases.

Another curious similarity is exemplified by a Star Person named "Barbara", who has had not one "walk-in" but three – very like the experiences of people who suffer with multiple personalities. Moreover, they play different roles. Her earlier Walk-ins had led her to break with her mother, but "the specific work of her third Walk-in was to heal her old family traumas". Once again, the thought arises that if the whole point of these extraterrestrials being on Earth rather than back home – wherever that may be – is to save our world from catastrophe, you would think they'd have better things to do than sort out family problems. That is particularly true in this case, as it is a problem for which they themselves were initially responsible. Barbara had told her husband that she was an extraterrestrial over a candlelit restaurant meal. He was unconvinced by her story, and after an argument walked out of the restaurant and her life. Perhaps it was necessary for the accomplishment of her "mission" that she be freed from the encumbrance of a husband. However, to achieve her own liberty at the expense of family disruption – she also told her little girl "You are not my daughter", which can't have been very nice for the child, seems a strange way for a superior race trying to improve the world to behave. On the other hand, it *is* quite characteristic of people facing a personal crisis.

If the Star People really are who they think they are, then this is probably the most important visitation from other worlds that we have experienced. One of them, Barbara Marx Hubbard from Washington DC, feels "a deep consciousness of having volunteered to come to this planet at this moment of evolutionary transition". If Star People like her are truly here to help our planet and its inhabitants solve our problems, it makes a welcome change from hostile

Private visions, such as this manifestation of the Sacred Heart of Jesus, play an important part in the spiritual life of mystics such as Teresa of Avila.

aliens who want to colonize us or enslave us or simply wipe us out so they can take our planet from us.

Providing the Star People are genuine, then we can at least say they are probably doing more good than harm. But some aspects of the Star People phenomenon make one uneasy: Some have already been mentioned: the concern with trivia, the lack of any marked progress. Another is the fact that virtually all of them are Americans. Perhaps the rest, scattered over the globe, are Sleeping Wanderers who don't yet know their heritage? Maybe if Brad and Francie Steiger's books were to be translated into Swahili, we'd see a change. If the Star People are here to change conditions on Earth, Africa needs them even more than the United States.

Secret societies, such as the Freemasons (seen here), the Rosicrucians and the Templars are often suspected of possessing "secret wisdom" handed down from one generation to the next.

WHY NOW?

If there are indeed millions of "Star People" living among us, and if they have been doing so all along, it is odd that it is only in the late twentieth century that they were revealed.

There may be a good reason for this. Many people have long believed that there are schools of occult teaching – the Rosicrucians, the Templars, the Masons, the Synarchy and hundreds more – which exist to guard a body of secret knowledge. This knowledge is held by just a few who carry on the tradition from one generation to the next, and who are, supposedly, biding their time until this or that happens. Could these be Star People?

Another point of view is that it is only now, when man has acquired so much new and dangerous knowledge, that it has become appropriate, even vital, for the rest of the universe to step in. Often UFO contactees are told by the aliens that Earth has become a source of concern for the rest of the galaxy.

A third alternative is that mankind has developed as far as is reasonable intellectually, and now the time has come for it to graduate to a more spiritual awareness of things. According to this view, which we will come across again in connection with the contactees, mankind is being prepared, gently and unobtrusively, for a total change.

Those who put forward this possibility point to "New Age" thinking, to the upsurge in concern for the environment, and to the widespread interest in alternative medicine, folklore and the like. Which is all very well, but if they could put a Star Person in the White House in 1801, it seems a pity they don't do it again.

"GODS AND SPACEMEN THROUGHOUT HISTORY"

In a book with this title, and six other volumes, author W Raymond Drake has collected evidence that extraterrestrial visits to our planet did not cease when the last of the "ancient astronauts" left, nor did they begin with the flying saucers of our own day. According to Drake, and many other researchers, there has been a succession of incidents which, rightly interpreted, point to the fact that these phenomena have been continuous throughout human history.

Unfortunately, that phrase "rightly interpreted" indicates the weakness of the case. Strange lights in the sky, accounts of aerial battles, ships seen in the heavens – these are all very intriguing, but we can never be certain that there isn't a more down-to-earth explanation.

Another perspective on this is that in former times we didn't have eyes to see. Perhaps it is only now, with our awareness of UFOs, that we can look back and see that they have been with us throughout history. Two French researchers, Olivyer and Boëdec, have searched through the *Histoires Admirables et memorables of Simon Goulart* (1543–1628), a French chronicler who made a record of all the remarkable events of the prior century in 1600. They found 93 unusual aerial phenomena:

July 4, 1554: there appeared in the air, about 10 p.m., in the region known as the High Palatinate of the Rhine, towards the Bohemian forest, two men in full armour, one considerably taller than the other, having on his belly a brightly shining star,

and a flaming sword in his hand, as also had the smaller one. They began a violent fight, at the end of which the smaller one was beaten down and could not move, whereupon a chair was brought for the victor, on which he sat, and never ceased to threaten with the sword he held in his hand the one who was lying at his feet, as if at any moment he would strike him. Finally, the two of them disappeared.

What are we to make of this remarkably detailed account? Unfortunately we are not told how many witnesses observed it, but I doubt if Goulart would have thought it worth recording if it was a single person's vision. It is hard to believe that everyday celestial objects – stars and planets – could have given rise to so circumstantial an account.

Several authors wanting to establish UFOs as an on-going historical phenomenon have seized on such accounts as evidence. Indeed, Olivyer

& Boëdec themselves subtitle their book "The UFO wave of 1500 to 1600". Belgian writer Christiane Piens compiled one of the more thoughtful collections. She concluded her 1977 book by writing:

In their broad outlines, the ancient cases are no different – apart from the frequency of their occurrence – from the modern ones. If we have succeeded in demonstrating their existence, we can no longer see the UFO phenomenon as a recent event. But this raises the complication that the beings (are they always the same species?) have been visiting us for many centuries without making official contact with mankind. We have to face the fact: the problem of non-contact is a great puzzle.

Since then, she tells me, she has come to be less sure about interpreting these sightings as evidence of extraterrestrial visitation. But that doesn't alter the fact

In July and August 1566, curious aerial phenomena were seen over Basel, Switzerland; the fact that they occurred at sunrise and sunset indicates a natural phenomenon, but others see them as early UFOs.

that these events occurred, and that chroniclers thought them worth recording. They serve as a reminder that strange things have been seen in Earth's skies throughout history.

As with the mysteries of ancient civilizations, these early UFOs present a problem on two levels. First, did they really take place as recorded? Second, if so, how are they to be interpreted? The dual problem is presented strikingly in the following case.

ALIENS BUZZ NICE

If certain "documents in the city's archives" can be taken at face value,

something happened in 1608 in the Italian town of Nizza, today the French city of Nice, which is strongly suggestive of a visit by extraterrestrial spacecraft.

Around 8pm on the August 5, 1608, the citizens of Nice saw three luminous shapes over the Baie des Anges, heading at high speed towards their city. Arriving in front of the citadel which overlooked the harbour, the three objects suddenly stopped and began to manoeuvre slowly at about 1 metre over the water. The low altitude and the slowness of their movement meant the watchers could examine the strange arrivals in detail. What they saw changed their curiosity into anxiety.

The machines were of long oval shape, flattened, and topped with a sort of mast. Hovering almost motionless, they caused the water beneath them to

seethe, giving off a dense orange-yellow vapour accompanied by an infernal noise. From one of the machines a living being emerged, followed by a second. They were approximately human in appearance, dressed in a kind of red outfit with what seemed to be silvery scales. Their heads were huge, and two luminous circular openings took the place of eyes. Holding two tubes attached to a kind of harness vertically in their arms, they plunged into the water up to their hips and proceeded to move round their machines for a couple of hours. Then, toward 10pm, the two visitors got back into their machine, and with a formidable rumbling all three raced off towards the east, becoming in a few seconds three little luminous points in the starry sky.

For the people of Nizza, these

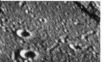

In 1608, mysterious flying machines approached the town of Nizza – today's Nice – on Italy's Mediterranean coast, alarming the populace.

From the harbour of Nizza (Nice), observers see the strange flying machines settle on the surface of the Baie des Anges.

portents could only be a warning from God. Terrified, they processed through the streets carrying the figure of Jesus, praying and imploring forgiveness for their sins, until the next day dawned with no further sign from their mysterious visitors.

But the visitors had not gone far. On August 22, they appeared further round the coast, at Genova. But the Genovese, who had heard what had happened at Nizza, reacted more violently. From the citadel, a salvo of artillery fire volleyed towards the three craft. Some 800 cannonballs were fired in hope of driving the visitors away. They did not cause the slightest damage to the machines though, nor distract them from their manoeuvres. However, it seems that the gunfire did discourage the occupants, for none emerged into the open on this occasion.

After about an hour, one of the machines left its companions and positioned itself over the town. The populace went into panic, and many injuries occurred. Several deaths were reported. Some were trampled by the crowds, others overcome by fear, but some also died as a result of radiations emitted by the vessel. Then, after a while, the machine rejoined the others, and they took off towards the east at top speed.

August 25, a single vessel appeared above Martigues, a fishing village close to Nizza, and manoeuvred overhead for an hour and a half. Two people got out, similar in appearance to the two who had been seen at Nizza. They flew round their craft. It seemed to the watchers as though they were engaged in a kind of airborne duel.

This was the last manifestation of the machines. But the following week there were abundant falls of coloured rain in

the area – red rain, like blood. It was certainly taken to be blood by the locals. who saw it as a warning from God, as any unusual event was interpreted at that time. A more prosaic explanation is that the local soil, rich in bauxite, has a red dust which may have been stirred up by the movements of the machines. For forty days churches were packed with crowds begging to be spared whatever disaster the mysterious machines might portend.

What are we to make of all this? The entries in the local archives, from which these accounts are taken, are couched in the language of the time, and much of the wording is ambiguous. This was an age when there was widespread belief in aerial visions. Impressive accounts of "armies in the sky" frequently occur in ancient chronicles, and doubtless ignorant people were apt to misinterpret natural happenings. But

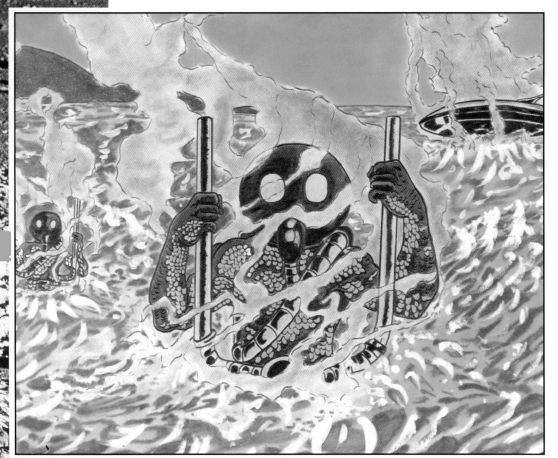

The strange occupants of the flying machines that invaded Nice in 1608.

these detailed observations seem to be more than that. Could so many people, in three separate locations, have imagined the whole affair, space ships and all, at a time when flight was not even considered as a possibility?

On the other hand, if these events really did take place as described, it is a remarkable event worthy of a place in history. Why haven't we heard more about it? One reason may be that the event is so ambiguous. There is no real interaction between the visitors and the Earthpeople, and the purpose of their visit remains obscure. None of it makes any sense.

The same is true of all the anomalous events which have been seized upon as evidence of continued extraterrestrial visits. There is no pattern, no evidence of purpose, and above all no contact.

But this was to change dramatically as the nineteenth century progressed. The growth of spiritualism, following on the experiences of the Fox sisters, led to new channels of communication with other worlds. For the most part this

communication was with the surviving dead, but some of it seemed to go further, and to open up ways to access other worlds.

THE GREAT MARTIAN TERROR

Mars is now as much a subject of conversation as politics or art. In Buenos Aires, Mexico, Caracas, as well as in Paris, St Petersburg, Budapest and Stockholm, the latest telescopic investigations are discussed, for it is known that this neighbouring world is actually approaching the earth …
The discovery of canal-like lines in the planet has led to the question of possible inhabitants of Mars, and of the probability of a future communication with them.

The words are those of the eminent French astronomer Camille Flammarion, writing in 1904. Who

should know better? For if people all over the world, in 1904 as in 1998, are talking about Mars, it is in large part his doing. In his popular books and articles, Flammarion for many years presented life on Mars as a scientific possibility. With so respectable an authority to guide them, every man or woman in the street felt authorized to contemplate the prospect that, any day now, we would find that we humans are not the only intelligent inhabitants of the universe.

One day in 1894, professor Auguste Lemaître of Geneva told his colleague Théodore Flournoy, professor of psychology at Geneva University, about a remarkable spirit medium, living in the same city, whose career he had been following for some six years. Flournoy, intrigued by what he heard, attended a seance with Catherine Elise Muller (named "Hélène Smith" in the accounts), which led to an investigation spread over several years. This culminated in a book which has become one of the great classics of psychological literature.

Catherine was a Swiss woman in her thirties, who had a responsible job in a store in Geneva. In personality she was intelligent, gifted, modest. In her leisure time, her chief activity was as a non-professional medium, who, in her seances, described what she saw, heard and what was communicated to her by rapped messages. Though Flournoy maintained a consistently sceptical attitude, openly disagreeing with his subject as to how her experiences should be interpreted, he retained her friendship and co-operation.

Catherine was privileged to receive a series of astonishing revelations which took her travelling, spiritually, in time and place. In one she was controlled by Victor Hugo, in another by a certain Leopold who was "really" Cagliostro. Later there was Marie Antoinette. What made them exceptional was that they were not simply "messages" from the past, but episodes in which Catherine actively participated – living scenes and events, vividly described as first-person experiences. This is just as true of her adventures on Mars as of those she enjoyed in ancient India or eighteenth-century France.

To explain how her Martian adventures started, we must go back to Flammarion, who had recently asserted:

What marvels the science of the future is keeping for our successors! Who will dare to deny that Martian humanity and terrestrial humanity may one day enter into communication one with the other?

Flammarion's ideas had been much discussed among Catherine's circle of friends. One day in 1894 professor Lemaître expressed the wish that in the future this might come about. This casual remark was clearly the trigger which sparked her space adventure, for she prefaced her first revelations with the words "Lemaître, here is what you wanted so much!"

What Catherine then proceeded to do, over a prolonged period, was to produce a whole chronicle of Martian adventures. Because she personally participated in them, they had all the clarity of first-hand descriptions. Some took place while she was asleep, some while she was awake, though doubtless in some form of altered state. So involved was Catherine in her Martian experiences, so continuous was the succession of episodes, that Flournoy came to the conclusion that *a part of Catherine was "living" her Martian existence every moment of the day or night.* Whenever she passed into another state – whether trance or sleep – she switched from her terrestrial existence to her Martian existence.

For example, on September 5, 1896, Catherine was awakened by a high wind which she thought might be dangerous for the flowers which she had put out on the windowsill of her bedroom. After rescuing her flowers, instead of going straight back to sleep she sat on her bed – except that now it was no longer a bed, it had become a bench. In the place of her window, looking out on the storm-swept streets of Geneva, she now saw before her a landscape crowded with exotic people. The bench was at the edge of a lake of a pinkish blue, with a bridge whose edges were transparent and constructed of yellow tubes, like organ pipes. She saw a male figure who was carrying a small machine like a lamp, which emitted flames and enabled him to fly. The vision lasted some 25 minutes, during all of which time Catherine was convinced she was awake, not asleep.

As episode succeeded episode, they

built up into a fairly comprehensive picture of life on Mars – how the Martians travelled, what their homes were like, and so on. What contributes to the power of the visions, though, was that so far as Catherine was concerned, any information was of only secondary interest. It was the events in which she was personally involved which were important for her. For example, we learn about Martian flowers from the detailed description she gave of the table ornaments at a great feast which took place in one of her visions. So vivid were these scenes that she was able to depict them in drawings.

But the most remarkable aspect of

her Martian experiences – the feature which makes her case of unique interest for our understanding of the human mind – is that Catherine learnt to speak the Martian language. This was revealed when, after having been inspired to draw a Martian house, she received what seemed to her a meaningless message:

Dode ne chi haudan te mechemetiche astane ke de me veche.

It wasn't till six weeks later that it was explained to her, by her Martian friends, what this message was telling her – that the house she had drawn

Catherine Muller's own drawing of herself, accompanied by her guardian angel.

A Martian script received by Catherine Muller in seance at Geneva in 1898: she learnt to speak the Martian language fluently.

same word with the same meaning. Nor were the words arbitrary, as though they had no meaning outside that particular utterance. It was a fully structured language with a coherent syntax. Indeed, it was precisely that fact which bothered Flournoy – the Martian language was structured in the same way as French, Catherine's native tongue.

The coincidence of Martians speaking a language structured in the same way as french was too great for Flournoy. He came to the conclusion that, incredible as it seemed, the language had been created by Catherine herself. Not, of course, in her conscious mind. This would have been virtually impossible for someone of her educational level, even given time, and there had been no time for preparation. The Martian language had made its appearance almost overnight. It was clear to Flournoy that it was a subconscious operation, but he found that even more significant than if she had indeed learnt it from her Martian friends. Catherine's command of the Martian language showed that her subconscious mind had the capability to create an entire grammatically consistent language and hold it in memory as surely as the language she had been speaking since she was a child.

Needless to say, this is not how Catherine herself saw the matter. Though she did not for a minute believe that she had visited Mars in her physical body, she was convinced that she had actually visited Mars in spirit. The clarity of her descriptions, the wealth of detail she was able to provide – which to Flournoy were evidence of her remarkable subconscious creativity – were to her convincing proof that she had indeed travelled to Mars in some manner. Apart from the interest for the psychologist of Catherine's Martian adventures, they are hardly less fascinating to the sociologist. For they were not an isolated phenomenon they occurred at a time when the "idea" of Mars was very much in the popular mind. There can be no doubt that they were inspired by the public context created by Flammarion and others.

belonged to Astane. He, it was revealed, had been the male figure she had seen with the mini-jet in her waking vision. From this point on, the Martian language made its appearance in her communications more and more.

The extraordinary thing is that Catherine used the Martian language consistently. There was no question of a "nonsense language", which she just gabbled to make an impression. After an interval of weeks she would use the

MRS CLEAVELAND

In 1901 the most eminent psychical researcher in America was probably James Hyslop, a professor of philosophy at Columbia University, New York. In that year he was contacted by the Reverend Cleaveland, a clergyman, whose wife had experienced some psychic phenomena which he thought Hyslop might find interesting.

Mrs Cleaveland (known as "Mrs Smead" in the accounts) had been having psychic experiences all her life, seeing apparitions, doing automatic writing and so on. In 1895, at about the same time that Catherine Muller started her Martian adventures, Mrs Cleaveland began to receive messages from some dead relatives. Three of them were her own children, and a fourth was a brother. Inevitably, one of the first things Mrs Cleaveland wanted to know was where they were. She received an utterly unexpected answer from one of her daughters, Maude. She learnt that "some spirits are on Earth and some are on other worlds".

Five weeks later the brother reported that Maude had gone to Mars. Soon Mrs Cleaveland was receiving messages from her, giving an account of her life on Mars. Compared with the vivid communications of Catherine Muller, these accounts were all on a very simple level. However, a detailed map was drawn showing various zones and naming them, and Maude confirmed that the canals of Mars were indeed constructed artificially by the Martians. This was very interesting, because the question of the canals of Mars was the subject of lively debate at that time. Indeed, articles on the subject had appeared earlier that very year in the *Atlantic Monthly*, though the Cleavelands insisted that they had not read them.

Maude was able to tell her mother more details of life on the planet and of the life-style of the Martians. Specimens of the Martian language were provided – "Mare" = man, "Maren" = men: "Kare" = woman, "Karen" = women. Though not nearly so developed as Catherine Muller's Martian tongue, it was structured like an earthly language – though in Maude Cleaveland's case it resembled English rather than French. Indeed, it resembled English more closely than it did the Martian language spoken by Catherine. Of course, just as there are many different languages spoken here on Earth, so it may be that there is more than one language spoken on Mars. However it is a curious coincidence that french-speaking Catherine's Martian language resembled french whereas English-speaking Mrs Cleaveland's Martian language was similar to English.

Maude gave a particularly interesting account of an airship, a propeller-driven vessel with flapping, inflated wings. The power source was electricity. This was a period when there was intense activity in aerial research, reflected in the "great airship scare" which swept through America at this time. Two years later the Wright brothers would demonstrate the first aeroplane, but all kinds of alternative methods of flight were being discussed, and it is interesting that Mrs Cleaveland's messages reflect this excitement.

In many ways life on Mars, as

Two Martians drawn by Mrs Cleaveland, as communicated by her daughter Maude who went to live on Mars after her death.

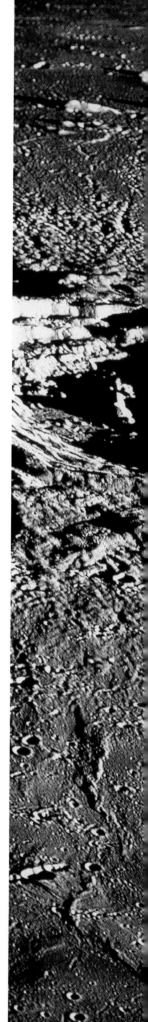

WILLS'S CIGARETTES.

IMAGINARY LANDSCAPE ON MARS.

At the start of the twentieth century, it was widely supposed that Mars was crossed by "canals", and this was confirmed by alleged communicators from the planet.

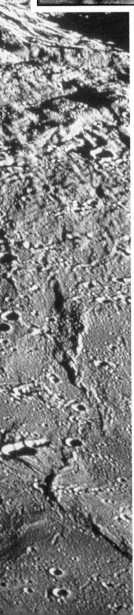

described by daughter Maude, was not so very different from life on Earth. The houses, furnishings, clothes and so on were variations on ours, just as they had been in Catherine Muller's descriptions. Nor would we have found it difficult to adapt to a Martian lifestyle. Aristocratic young humans might not feel too happy about having to work in the fields, but all young Martians were required to do so until they married.

Though Hyslop was apt to be a believer when it came to communication from spirits, he was not so credulous when it was a matter of messages from otherworldly beings. Like Flournoy in Geneva, he came to the conclusion that these message came from a secondary personality of Mrs Cleaveland:

> We find in such cases evidence that we need not attribute fraud to the normal consciousness, and we discover automatic processes of mentation that may be equally acquitted of fraudulent intent while we are also free from the obligation to accept the phenomena at their assumed value. Their most extraordinary characteristic is the extent to which they imitate the organizing intelligence of a normal mind, and the perfection of their impersonation of spirits.

HELENE PREISWERK

A third person from the same period who reported contact with alien beings was another young Swiss woman, Hélène Preiswerk, both a cousin and a patient of the Zurich psychologist Carl Gustav Jung. In 1899 Helene was a somewhat disturbed 15½ year old girl. Her family history included many relatives who had experienced hallucinations and other visionary experiences, somnambulism, prophetic utterances, hysterical episodes and nervous heart attacks. Though she herself displayed no outwardly hysterical symptoms, Helene was moody, absent-minded and distracted.

Like Catherine in Geneva, Helene had found a distraction from her unsatisfying home life in spiritualism. She, too, turned out to be an excellent medium. Jung was invited to witness for himself the states of "somnambulism" in which Helene performed remarkable feats of impersonation.

Even when not in spirit trance, Helene would report visits by "spirits" – "shining white figures who detached themselves from the foggy brightness,

wrapped in white veil-like robes ..." They were "generally of a pleasant nature", but she also had terrifying demonic visions. Good or evil, she accepted them as the sort of thing a spirit medium must expect to encounter in the course of her activities. She was very happy in what she believed to be her true vocation, and she made it clear to Jung that she was unshakeably convinced of the reality of her visions:

> I do not know if what the spirits say and teach me is true, nor do I know if they really are the people they call themselves; but that my spirits exist is beyond question. I see them before me, I can touch them. I speak to them about everything I wish, as naturally as I'm talking to you. They must be real.

Not surprisingly, she refused to accept that these experiences meant that she was in any way ill. She was hurt by Jung's scepticism, so, like Flournoy had with Catherine, he learnt to be discreetly diplomatic with his subject.

Helene's trances frequently involved journeys to spirit worlds in the beyond – "that space between the stars which people think is empty, but which really contains countless spirit worlds". Some of these she was able to describe:

she told us all the peculiarities of the star-dwellers; they have no godlike souls, as men have, they pursue no science, no philosophy, but in the technical arts they are far more advanced than we are. Thus, flying machines have long been in existence on Mars; the whole of Mars is covered with canals. The canals are artificial lakes and are used for irrigation.

Helene's account on life on Mars is less detailed than that of Catherine Muller or Maude Cleaveland. But unlike them, she had one otherworldly experience while on Earth:

She once returned from a railway journey in an extremely agitated state. We thought at first that something unpleasant must have happened to her; but finally she pulled herself together and explained that "a star-dweller had sat opposite her in the train". From the description she gave of this being, I recognized an elderly merchant I happened to know, who had a rather unsympathetic face.

Subsequently, Jung tells us, Helene Preiswerk abandoned spiritualism, and nothing more was heard of her "star-dwellers".

MIREILLE AND THE ELECTRIC FIELDS

In 1895 – the same year as Mrs Cleaveland began to receive her messages from Mars – the noted French researcher Colonel Albert de Rochas was, like Jung, asked to help a family friend. Mireille, now age 45, had been known to him since childhood. She had a troublesome ailment, and knowing that he had success with healing by hypnosis, she hoped he could help her.

The therapy was successful, and in return, Mireille agreed to help him with his experimental work, having proved herself a good and willing hypnotic subject. Though intelligent she was not highly educated, but she moved in circles where current ideas were discussed. Although not herself interested in the paranormal, she would

certainly have heard her friends discussing subjects such as the possibility of extraterrestrial life.

In one of her hypnotic sessions, she described how she seemed to be rising in space, which she said was brightly luminous and peopled with "phantoms". Among these she noted a childhood friend, Victor, who had been dead for ten years. During subsequent sessions she told of visits to Mars and other planets. She was unable to give detailed descriptions, only vague references to the canals which, as we have seen, were an everyday source of discussion at the time. All she could say of the Martians was that they were physically superior to Earthpeople but less intelligent.

In fact, nothing very out of the ordinary occurred until the day when, instead of Mireille telling of her own experiences, she seemed to be possessed by Victor, who presented himself in the role of Mireille's guide and protector. He told de Rochas that he had nearly "lost" Mireille, owing to the electric fields she had to penetrate in order to reach Mars.

From that point on, Mireille served almost entirely as Victor's channel of communication. De Rochas was always immediately aware when Mireille had given place to Victor. Normally he would hold Mireille's hand while she was in trance. Victor didn't think it right for two males to hold hands though, and as soon as he took over Mireille's body, the hand was withdrawn. While Mireille didn't smoke, Victor did. Moreover, de Rochas found it awkward to explain to Victor why he was wearing female clothing.

There may have been another reason why Victor found it embarrassing to hold hands. Describing life on other planets, he explained that there it is arms above all which are the organs of affection, and manual expressions of tender feelings are the rule. Consequently the arms tend to become highly developed, and are sometimes mistaken for wings when angels and other spirits are seen. Which was a stupid idea anyway, Victor derisively pointed out, for ethereal beings such as angels and spirits had no need of physical wings to fly!

Practical comments of this kind were typical of Victor's no-nonsense communications. De Rochas soon found it quite natural to hold conversations with

Victor – speaking through Mireille – as if he was indeed the living, intelligent being he claimed to be. This led to some amusing misunderstandings:

One day I revealed to Victor my doubts as to the reality of his existence outside the imagination of Mireille. I told him that what made me suspicious was that the alleged communicators, though they might be talking about the same subject, often contradicted one another.
"Happily", Victor replied, "your doubts as to whether I exist don't prevent me existing! As for the matter of contradiction, you need to distinguish carefully where the revelations are coming from. If they are from a spirit which is more or less detached from its astral body, it can and often will take for reality what is actually no more than the objectivization of its own thoughts and memories. This is why every ecstatic has visions which conform to his own religious beliefs."
"You are mistaken if you think there exists any profound difference between the world of the living and that of the dead, or any hiatus separating them.
The spirit life continues beyond the tomb with no more transition than if, in the life of flesh, the inhabitants of a house being at first gathered in a ground-floor room dimly lit by narrow windows, a few should separate from the others and go upstairs to where the rooms are illuminated with light".

Though Victor put up strong arguments for his existence, de Rochas retained his doubts. But as in the case of Catherine Muller's Martian language, though the facts may not be what they seem to be, that does not make them any the less remarkable. If, as de Rochas suspected, Victor was a projection created by Mireille's own unconscious, it was remarkable that this poorly-educated lady possessed the experience to support his fantasy existence with such clearly thought-out arguments.

In the 1890s, Mars was an idea whose time had come. It inspired not only scientific speculation but also individual fantasy claimed as actual experience. If this was true of "the great Martian terror", we must ask ourselves whether it may be equally true of other claimed experiences which echo prevailing notions?

THE MARTIAN MYTH

The fiction-writers knew they were creating a mythical Mars peopled by mythical Martians. The spiritualists believed they were telling the truth about Mars, though most of us will probably agree with Flournoy, Jung, Hyslop and de Rochas that we need look no farther than the limitless creativity of the subconscious human mind. As for the scientists, though they based their speculations on fact and observation, they could sometimes be just as wide of the mark as the others. The American astronomer Percival Lowell believed that Mars was criss-crossed with canals, but the introduction of more powerful telescopes has shown them to be delusory. The Martians that Flammarion hoped we would one day meet have been found to no longer exist, and probably never did.

But the Martian myth is more than a tissue of wishes and imaginings. The fact that Catherine Muller, Mrs Cleaveland, Helene Preiswerk and Mireille could each create a personal Mars of the mind is an impressive tribute to the human imagination. Moreover, the myth has shown a remarkable survival value. In France the term "Martien" is virtually a synonym for extraterrestrials. When, in 1963, Michel Carrouges wrote his telling study of the UFO phenomenon, he entitled it *Les Apparitions de Martiens* in tribute to the myth.

So, although the term "Martian" was frequently used by the French during the great wave of sightings they experienced in 1954, this did not mean that they really believed the UFOs were of Martian origin. However, in that same year, there was published in England one of the few UFO books to claim that the extraterrestrials do really come from Mars. An amateur ornithologist named Cedric Allingham was bird-watching in the north of Scotland when he saw and photographed a UFO and actually met its pilot, who told him he came from Mars. The photograph Allingham

took, as the Martian walked back to his spaceship, shows a very human-like being, not at all like the monsters dreamed up by the science fiction illustrators.

Cedric Allingham disappeared from view after his book was published, and indeed there are allegations that he never actually existed. Another theory persisted, that he existed under the name of Patrick Moore, a popular English astronomer with a reputation for practical joking. However, Moore has always denied this allegation, and so the possibility remains that this is a

genuine photograph. If so, it is probably the only photograph of a Martian in existence.

Even if the Martians do not exist outside our own imaginations, we should not belittle them. They have provided us with a wonderful "straw man" to embody our hopes and our fears. H G Wells's great fantasy still has the power to spark our imaginations, as demonstrated by the one of the latest re-interpretations, the blockbuster movie, *Independence Day*.

For Catherine Muller and the others,

LEFT: *In France, Martians were the archetypal aliens, so the term covered all extraterrestrials.*

In 1954 Cedric Allingham, an ornithologist, took this unique photograph of a Martian near Lossiemouth in northern Scotland.

The success of the film Independence Day, *and others like it, is proof that the myth of hostile aliens is still a powerful source of anxiety.*

the Martians symbolized the wider, richer realms that lie beyond the reach of our earthly senses. It seems that we all, subconsciously, crave the excitement which Barthel and Brucker – analysing the French 1954 wave – named *La Grande Peur Martienne*, the great Martian terror!

THE MARTIAN STEREOTYPE

In 1997, American writer Patrick Huyghe published *A Field Guide to Extraterrestrials*, which seeks to do for flying saucer occupants what bird-spotters' guides do for birds. In other words, to identify and classify the various types of alien that witnesses

have reported so that we too – should we be fortunate enough to meet one – will know with what species we are dealing.

Huyghe is careful to point out that he can pass on to us only what the witnesses themselves report. Often they were alone when they had their sighting, frequently they were taken by surprise, understandably they might be alarmed and confused. The testimony on which he bases his categories is of uncertain reliability. But though that might tend to make his book of limited value if one encountered an extraterrestrial – one cannot, somehow, picture oneself rapidly flipping through the pages till we identify our companion as a "Humanoid, Short Non-Grey, Variant 5" – it shows that a kind of consensus has come about as to what UFO occupants look like. This

inevitably leads to the feeling that this what they *should* look like, which in turn has the result that this is what people who fantasize do see, or think they see. It is interesting to note that this process also applies to visions of the Virgin Mary, seance-room materializations and other perceived beings.

The imagination of the science fiction writers of the 1920s and 1930s was matched only by that of their illustrators. The aliens they drew range from humanoid look-alikes to creatures with no pretensions to resemble Earthpeople. Tentacles were very popular with the monsters. Some of the humanoids differ from us in having more arms or fewer eyes. Giant insects and fish-scaled mammals occur from time to time, but the preference is for various forms of reptilian lizardry. Comparing the science-fiction

In H G Wells's The First Men in the Moon, *space traveller Cavor is taken prisoner by insect-like inhabitants of the Moon.*

essential part of him … His brain grows continually larger, at least so far as the portions engaging in mathematics are concerned; they bulge ever larger and seem to suck all life and vigour from the rest of his frame.

These "consensus" aliens generally possess two eyes, though they tend to be larger than ours and are often described as "wrap-around". Since Nature decided that for most species on Earth, two is the most practical number of eyes – whether birds, mammals, fish and insects, two eyes is the norm rarely departed from – we may suppose that the same reasoning would apply elsewhere. The eyes are positioned as ours are. No alien has eyes in the sides of its head like our birds, or on stalks, though this is sometimes found on science fiction monsters. There is less uniformity with regard to the other organs. Various combinations of ears, nose and mouth, or the absence thereof, have been reported. Where they are present, they are invariably located where ours are. They rarely have hair.

Although Wells had made his Martians closer to cephalopods than to anything resembling a human, in *When the Atoms Failed* (1930) by John W Campbell Junior, artist Wesso (Hans

illustrations with the aliens depicted in Huyghe's book, there isn't much to choose between them. Both offer predictable variations on the human body, such as one might expect to find on a nearly-parallel world, but also monsters which are, more often than not, extrapolations from earth species. The diversity of life on Earth is more than sufficient to provide all the models of otherworldly life we could wish for.

There is one species, however, which has gradually established itself as the dominant alien type. It is an essentially humanoid entity. It has a body which presumably contains the essential organs, to which are joined two legs for walking on and two arms with which to perform tasks, topped by a head which

appears to house the senses and the organs of communication. The head is generally larger in proportion to the body than with adult humans, often giving this species the look of the unborn human foetus. Since aliens are generally perceived as being more highly developed intellectually than ourselves, their heads may be larger to accommodate greater brain capacity. Perhaps it is with them as with the creatures discovered by *The First Men in the Moon* in H G Wells's 1901 novel:

If, for example, a Selenite is destined to be a mathematician …his brain grows, or at least the mathematical faculties of his brain grow, and the rest of him only so much as is necessary to sustain this

"WABBLING JELLIES OF KNOWLEDGE."

Worker Selenites carry an intellectual who is no longer capable of walking due to his huge brain.

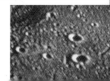

¶ *They obeyed in some little trepidation, drawing near the strange conveyance and stopping as a small square opening appeared in the side nearest them*

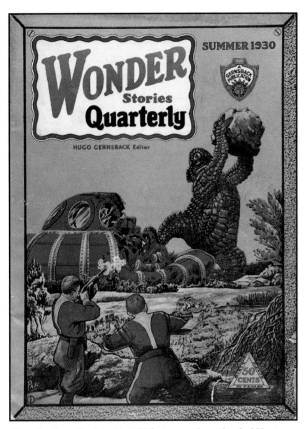

Travellers from Earth in this 1930 fiction are alarmed to find Neptune inhabited by powerful creatures who trample on their spacecraft.

with four limbs, body, head and the usual sense organs. But are they necessarily right? Those other worlds might have conditions vastly different from Earth's, and yet be inhabited. In which case we would encounter creatures whose forms are adapted to life there. They might be much bigger or much smaller, depending on the force of gravity. Even if we assume an atmosphere much like ours, variations in atmospheric pressure might necessitate enormously larger lungs or even some other system for taking in whatever chemicals is necessary to sustain life. Very slight differences in the atmosphere would affect sight and sound, requiring appropriate modification of the sense organs. The disproportionately enormous ears of the extraterrestrials shot at by the Sutton family at Hopkinsville, Kentucky, in August 1955, could mean that they come from a planet where sound needs to be amplified more than here on Earth.

Overall, neither the science fiction illustrators nor the claimed witnesses have departed very far from existing species on Earth. Yet they might well have done, without undue extravagance. For example, humans have often been reported as "seeing" with parts of their anatomy other than the eyes. Biologists scoff, since even if visual perceptions could be obtained by the stomach, as has been claimed, it is difficult to see how those perceptions could be transmitted to the brain and processed like images from the eyes. But the concept of perception distributed over the entire body is not totally extravagant, just as alternative methods of fuelling the body – making use of quite different chemicals – might reflect conditions on another world.

If the physical configuration of the consensus aliens remains surprisingly close to our own, the same is true of their behaviour. When Catherine Muller and her contemporaries described the Martians, they never implied that their conduct was in any way different from ours. We have seen that, by and large, the same is true of the science fiction writers. Often, they produced sophisticated theories about aliens, seeing them as dispassionate superior species to whom we Earthpeople are little more than cattle. In Eando Binder's The *Impossible World* [1939], the invading intelligences "brainwash" Earthpeople with sophisticated technical instruments, as sinister terrestrial forces – from Chinese communists to the CIA – are often accused of doing. The psychology of the aliens is frequently presented in the same manner as the evil scientist who wants to take over the world in terrestrial fantasy stories: cold, calculating, unfeeling.

As we shall see, this is also the

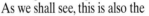

Waldemar Wessolowski) perceives the Martians as gnome-like creatures. They are humanoid in configuration, with disproportionate heads and staring eyes, very much as described more recently by abductees. Unlike the later ones, though, they have very prominent ears. The alien invaders depicted by Leo Morey for Harl Vincent's *Microcosmic Buccaneers* (1929) are even more similar to today's abductors. They have human shape, big heads, and staring eyes, but no nose or mouth. When they land on Earth and see some Earthpeople watching them, they wave their arms in salutation just as we do!

Some exobiologists – those who speculate about life on other worlds – hold that, to produce life at all, conditions comparable to Earth's are needed. This seems an unjustifiably anthropocentric view, but if they are right, then it would not be surprising if life developed there along more or less similar lines. Aliens would then be more or less similar to ourselves – bipedal,

LEFT: *Visiting aliens from 1929 were much like the ones seen 20 years later, but far friendlier!*

More than 20 years later, aliens are still seen as monsters, as in this poster for a 1953 movie.

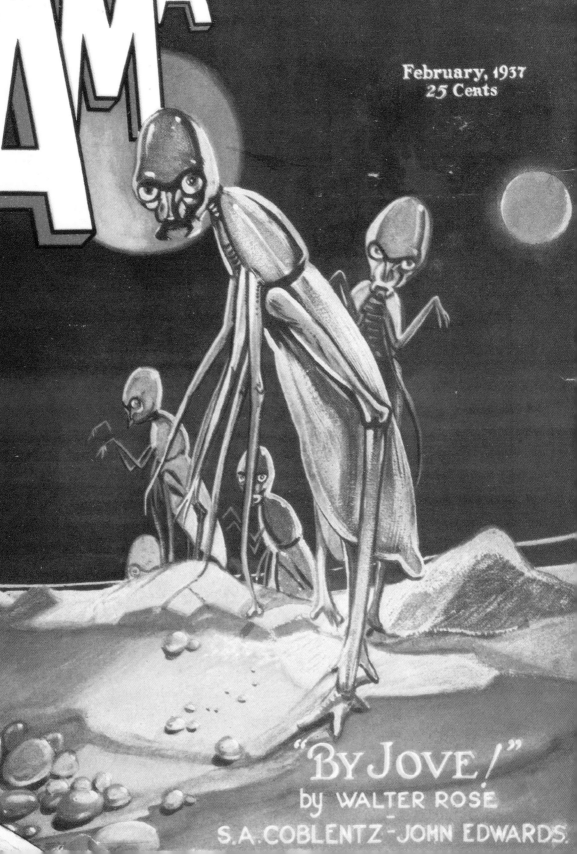

AMAZING STORIES

February, 1937
25 Cents

"BY JOVE!"
by WALTER ROSE
—
S. A. COBLENTZ – JOHN EDWARDS

At their home in Hopkinsville, Kentucky, in 1955, the Sutton family are besieged by alien creatures who are not hurt even when hit by bullets.

it as such. Some would argue that so widespread a consensus must reflect reality. To others, it is a tribute to man's genius for mythmaking.

In 1979, the French researcher Eric Zurcher published a survey of extraterrestrial beings, entitled: *Les Apparitions d' Humanoïds.* He presents a study of their morphology, dress, activity and comportment. What strikes him is, first, how human-like most aliens are; and second, how they reflect human preoccupations – a legionnaire sees Ufonauts dressed in khaki and carrying backpacks; a farmer sees Ufonauts examining plants; a retired soldier sees a Ufonaut carrying a sword!

This doesn't make much sense, until you look at the aliens in context with folklore. Traditional entities like the Irish *leprechaun* and the Breton *korrigan* not only resemble aliens physically, but also seem to mimic human behaviour. Yet they do so in the way that seems to be most appropriate to the age in which they are seen. Similarly, the illustrations to Hugo Gernsback's science-fiction pulps could not have been created at the time of Catherine Muller and HG Wells. Zurcher suggests:

Everything takes place ... as if the key themes of mankind's dreams are somehow kept in some kind of store, from which the phenomenon of the flying saucer can draw directly on its models and its manifestations.

He points out, we are close to Jung's notion of a "collective unconscious" with its universal archetypes. Jung himself recognized this when he subtitled his own study of flying saucers "a modern myth of things seen in the skies". We began this book with the suggestion that otherworldly beings visited Earth long before human history: we conclude with the suggestion that we should think of them as outside history, timeless beings embedded in the human subconscious.

impression given to those who report being abducted onto extraterrestrial spacecraft. They feel themselves to be guinea pigs, involuntarily assisting the aliens in their research. However, the contactees of the preceding era presented quite a different picture of caring, sensitive beings, concerned about the way we are treating our planet and offering their services to help us do better.

These fluctuations in the way we perceive our extraterrestrial visitors may reflect reality. Perhaps different Earthpeople are meeting different aliens. Alternatively, perhaps they reflect our own attitudes, our hopes, expectations and fears. What is most remarkable, though, is the fact that we are able to perceive them at all. It is by no means certain that people from other worlds exist, yet any schoolchild, invited to draw a space person, will reach for a pencil and draw a space person and you and I would at once recognize

LEFT: *Giant insects featured in science fiction pulps like this 1937 story, and were a favourite of Hollywood horror movies, but are a comparative rarity in UFO reports.*

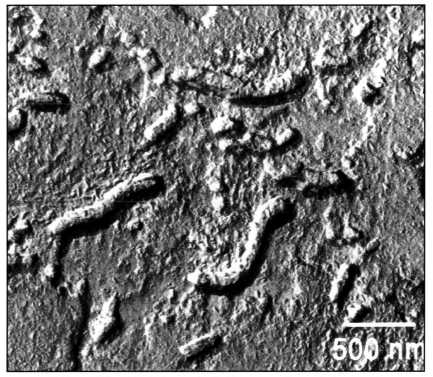

Evidence of life on Mars? Microscopic tube-like structures from a Martian meteorite could be fossilized bacteria-like organisms.

INDEX

Picture Credits

The publishers would like to thank the following sources for their kind permission to reproduce the pictures in this book:

The Bridgeman Art Library, London; Corbis/Bettmann-UPI, Everett/*The X-Files, Independence Day* TCF/Centropolis 1996, *Invaders From Mars* Edward L. Alperson 1953; Mary Evans Picture Library; Fortean Picture Library/ Klaus Aarsleff, Dr Elmar R. Gruber, Debbie Lee; Science Photo Library/NASA; South American Pictures/Tony Morrison; David Tarn

Every effort has been made to acknowledge correctly and contact the source and/or copyright holder of each picture, and Carlton Books Limited apologizes for any unintentional errors or omissions which will be corrected in future editions of this book.

About the Author

Hilary Evans is an acknowledged authority on UFOs, extra-terrestrial experiences and the paranormal. He writes and lectures on anomaly research, psychical research, folklore and myth, and related subjects. He is a member of the Society for Psychical Research, the American Society for Psychical Research; the Society for Scientific Exploration; the Association for the Scientific Study of Anomalous Phenomena and the Folklore Society. He has written books on many aspects of anomaly research, notably *Intrusions*; *Visions, Apparitions and Alien Visitors*; *Gods, Spirits, and Cosmic Guardians*; *Frontiers of Reality*; and *Alternate States of Consciousness*. He is the author of four books on UFOs: *UFOs, the Greatest Mystery*; *The Evidence for UFOs*; *UFOs 1947–1987* and *UFOs 1947–1997* and has published many articles on these subjects. He was also writer–consultant for *Almanac of the Uncanny* and several other Reader's Digest publications. He lives in London.